Dorset Dishes

by

KATE EASLEA

50p

Published by Paul Cave Publications Ltd., 13 Portland Street, Southampton

Other Books by Kate Easlea:
"Cooking In Hampshire — Past and Present"
"Come To Dinner"
"Simple Sweets and Candies"
"New Meals For Old"
"Baking with Botley Mill"

Printed by Brown & Son (Ringwood) Ltd., Crowe Arch Lane, Ringwood, Hampshire.

Published May, 1979
ISBN 0-86146-004-9

INTRODUCTION

I have been encouraged in the preparation of this little book of Dorset recipes by the continued interest shown in the book "Cooking in Hampshire Past & Present," which has been reprinted eight times since it was first published in 1973. Dorset and Hampshire are associated in so many ways, not least by the recent boundary changes.

I am grateful to the many members of Women's Institutes who have assisted me in searching out the recipes and to the friends who have helped in testing many of the dishes.

The very old recipes have been included for interest only.

Kate Easlea

Abbreviations

tsp.	=	teaspoon
dessp.	=	dessertspoon
tbsp.	=	tablespoon
oz.	=	ounce
lb.	=	pound
fl. oz.	=	fluid ounce

Weights and Measures

1 ounce	=	28 grammes, approximately
1 pound	=	500 grammes or ½ kilogramme, approximately
2lbs. 3 ozs.	=	1,000 grammes or 1 kilogramme
¼ pint	=	5 fluid ounces, 1 gill or 8 tablespoonsful
1 pint	=	20 fluid ounces or ½ litre
1¾ pints	=	35 fluid ounces or 1 litre
1 teacup	=	¼ pint or 1 gill
1 standard egg (size 4)	=	2 ounces

Oven Temperatures

	Electric Setting		*Gas Mark*
Very cool	250°F	130°C	½
Cool	275°F	140°C	1
	300°F	150°C	2
Very moderate	325°F	170°C	3
Moderate	350°F	180°C	4
Fairly hot	375°F	190°C	5
	400°F	200°C	6
Hot	425°F	220°C	7
Very hot	450°F	230°C	8

SOUPS, STARTERS AND SAVOURIES

A soup needs a good stock.
A stock pot stood on the stove in farmhouse and cottage kitchens.
All scraps of meat and root vegetables were added and the pot was boiled every day to keep the contents sweet. (The modern equivalent is a stock cube!)
Many savoury soups were made from next to nothing and helped to feed hungry families.

Marrow and Potato Soup

1 medium marrow
5-6 medium potatoes
1 large onion
2 ozs. margarine or butter
pepper and salt
pinch of celery seeds
or 1 stick of chopped celery
3 pints stock
1 dessp. small sago
½ pint milk
variations:-
artichokes, turnips, carrots, pumpkin etc.
chopped parsley

Method

Skin and slice marrow, removing seeds.
Peel and slice potatoes and onion.
Melt fat, add vegetables and sweat them, covered for 3-4 minutes until soft.
Add stock and seasonings.
Bring to the boil and simmer until cooked.
Sieve or blend and return to pan with milk.
Bring to the boil, sprinkle in sago and cook until sago becomes transparent.
Serve hot, sprinkled with parsley.

Hotch Potch Soup

This is well named as it can contain small amounts of any vegetables.

½ carrot
½ turnip or swede
2 pints mutton or other white broth
1 small onion
1 small cauliflower
¼ pint green peas
1 tsp. chopped parsley
seasoning

Method

Peel and dice carrot, turnip and onion.
Simmer in broth until tender.
Cook cauliflower separately in boiling salted water
Divide into pieces and add to broth.
Stir in peas and cook until soft.
Season well and add parsley.

Soup With Lettuce

This is a very old recipe from the 17th century and is for interest only.

Take 6 Quarts of Water, 4 or 5 Cabbage Lettuces, a Peck of Green Pease the older the better, a bunch of Mint, a little whole Pepper; boil it several hours till it will walk thro' a Cullender; then take a pint of young Pease, one Silesia Lettice chopp'd small, just give it a boil up together, then throw in a good Piece of Butter and a litte salt, a little Onion to those who like I think three Lettuces if large ones enough.'

Regalia Of Cucumbers

Outdoor ridge cucumbers can be used in this recipe, but should be peeled.

6 large cucumbers
salt
oil
1 large onion, sliced
2 rashers chopped bacon
flour
red wine or vinegar
pepper

Method

Cut cucumbers into 1'' slices and sprinkle with salt.
Leave half an hour, then drain and rinse well.
Fry onion and bacon in a little oil until brown. Drain.
Fry cucumbers until brown in a clean pan. Drain liquor.
Add onion and toss in wine.
Add pepper and bacon.

Boiled Cheese

Useful in sandwiches or spread on toast.

4 ozs. mild cheese
2 pieces butter, walnut size
2 tbsps. cream
1 egg

Method

Cut cheese in slices.
Put in a pan with butter and cream.
Bring very slowly to the boil, stirring until smooth.
Add beaten egg and stir quickly before putting into a dish.

Green Butter

2 ozs. butter
2 ozs. anchovies (soaked in milk)
handful of parsley
pinch bicarbonate of soda
hot toast

Method

Boil parsley with soda in water to cover until quite soft.
Sieve with anchovies (drained).
Mix with butter and beat well.
Serve on hot toast.

Dorset Flan or Dorset Delight

This is a savoury flan with a difference. Serve it with 'Darzet' watercress.

6 ozs. shortcrust pastry
4 ozs. thin ham
3 eggs
½ pint milk
1 dessp. semolina or ground rice
seasoning

Method

Line a flan or pie dish with pastry.
Cover base with ham.
Break two whole eggs on top.
Blend semolina or ground rice with the other egg and milk to a thin batter.
Season and pour carefully over ham and eggs.
Bake 20-30 minutes at gas 6 or 400°F.

An Old Recipe for Cheese Tart

'Take a cruste and yuche deep in a dysshe Take yǒlkes of rawe egges and strong cheese and mix it with the yolkes together Add thereto powder ginger. sweetening. saffron and salte Put ye eggs on ye cruste. bake it and serve it forth'

FISH DISHES

The coastal stretches of Dorset are well known for high quality fish.
Weymouth is famous for red mullet and most fishing villages have crabs and mackerel for sale.

Devilled Dorset Crab

12 ozs. crab meat
4 ozs. fresh breadcrumbs
2 ozs. melted butter or margarine
3 tbsps. lemon juice
2 tsps. Worcester sauce
1 tsp. made mustard
salt and cayenne pepper
extra lemon juice

Method

Mix all ingredients together reserving one tablespoon of breadcrumbs and one tablepoon of fat.
Place mixture in shallow oven dishes or crab shells.
Sprinkle with rest of breadcrumbs and add melted fat.
Bake 15 minutes at gas 5 or 375°F.
Serve hot, sprinkled with lemon juice.

Baked Mackerel

Mackerel should only be used when it is very fresh. The skin should be shiny and bright.

4 fresh mackerel, cleaned
salt
lemon juice
¼ pint cider
2 tbsps. wine or cider vinegar
2 bay leaves
4 black peppercorns
chopped parsley

Method

Make cuts on each side of fish.
Rub with salt and lemon juice.
Put in dish and pour over cider and vinegar.
Add bay leaves and peppercorns.
Bake uncovered 15-20 minutes at gas 7 or 425°F.
Sprinkle with parsley and leave to cool.

Stargazy Pie

The decoration of the heads may be omitted but is a traditional feature.

4 mackerel or herrings
salt and pepper
chopped parsley
4 tbsps. fresh breadcrumbs
4 rashers streaky bacon
4 eggs
¼ pint thin cream
or 2 tbsps. tarragon vinegar
6-8 ozs. shortcrust pastry
sprigs of parsley

Method

Wash fish, open them up and remove bones, but keep heads.
Lay fish flat and season with salt, pepper and parsley. Roll up.
Sprinkle buttered oven dish with crumbs.
Lay in two fish and cover with more crumbs. Add rest of fish.
Top with bacon and pour over beaten eggs mixed with cream or vinegar.
Roll pastry and make lid to cover dish.
Make holes in centre and insert heads (optional).
Bake 30-40 minutes at gas 7 or 425°F.
Place sprig of parsley in fish mouths before serving.

Stewed Carp

Dorset has one main river, the Stour, and two main streams, the Piddle and Frome. Carp is fished from both river and streams.

4 carp, well cleaned
claret
bundle of thyme and winter savoury
6 sliced onions
3-4 chopped anchovies
2 cloves
1 blade of mace
4 peppercorns
pinch ground ginger
pinch ground nutmeg
strip of lemon rind
2 egg yolks
a little melted butter

Method

Put fish in a pan and prick their tails.
Almost cover with claret.
Add herbs, onions, anchovies, spices and lemon rind.
Cover and stew until cooked, turning twice.
Strain liquor and thicken with egg yolks in a double pan, without boiling.
Fold in butter and pour over fish.

Stuffed Herrings

Mackerel can also be used in this recipe.

4 fresh herrings with roes
4 tbsps. fresh breadcrumbs
1 tbsp. melted butter or margarine.
1 tsp. anchovy essence
1 tsp. chopped onion
salt and pepper
mustard butter –
    1 oz. butter
    1 tsp. dry mustard
    1 tsp. lemon juice

Method

Wash and dry fish and remove heads.
Split open and remove backbones.
Cook roes in a little boiling water.
Drain and chop.
Mix roes with crumbs, melted fat, anchovy essence, onion and seasoning.
Stuff fish and close.
Brush with fat and bake 20 minutes gas 4 or 350°F
Sauce – Mix butter, mustard and lemon juice.
Form into a roll and cut pats to serve with hot stuffed fish.

Weymouth Red Mullet

Red mullet gets its name from its pink skin. It is in season from May to September.

4 red mullet
seasoned flour
1 small sliced onion
1 tbsp. chopped parsley.
1 tbsp. chopped fennel
4 chopped mushrooms
4 tbsps. sherry or wine
butter
salt
pinch cayenne pepper
to serve –
    melted butter flavoured with anchovy essence
squeeze of lemon

Method

Butter an oven dish.
Place fish in dish and cover with rest of ingredients.
Cover with buttered paper or foil.
Bake ½ hour at gas 4 or 350°F.
Serve with melted butter and anchovy essence.
Sprinkle with lemon juice.

MEAT and POULTRY DISHES

Lamb from the Dorset chalk hills, where curlews circle over flocks of curly coated sheep.

Spicy Dorset Lamb Pie

8 ozs. shortcrust pastry made with
 lamb dripping and seasoning
¾-1 lb. cold cooked lamb, cut in small pieces
seasoning
½ lb. coarsely chopped cooking apples
little sugar
nutmeg
few currants or chopped prunes
finely grated lamb suet
milk for glaze

Method

In a pie dish pack meat and apples in layers with dried fruit, sugar and nutmeg.
Add seasoning and cover with suet.
No water is required.
Roll out pastry and cover dish.
Brush with milk and bake about 35 minutes at gas 7 or 425°F.

Country Baked Port Chops with Apple

1 lb. cooking apples
1 large chopped onion
1 tbsp. sugar
1 level tsp. sage or savory
4 pork chops, trimmed
¼ pint cider
seasoning
4 tbsps. browned breadcrumbs
4 tbsps. grated cheese
2 ozs. butter or margarine
garnish –
 1 large apple in rings
 little butter or margarine

Method

Peel, core and slice apples into greased pie dish.
Add onion and sprinkle with sugar and herbs.
Place chops on top and pour in cider.
Season well.
Mix crumbs with cheese and sprinkle over chops.
Dot with fat and bake 45 minutes at gas 6 or 400°F until chops are tender and top is crisp.
Fry apple rings in fat and arrange on top.

Fricacee of Veal or Pork

A fricacee is a dish cooked with a rich cream sauce. The modern spelling is Fricassee.

1 ½ lbs. lean veal or pork, diced
2 medium onions, sliced
¾ pint white stock
pinch thyme, marjoram and parsley
10 white peppercorns
2 cloves
1 oz. butter
¼ pint white wine or cider
extra herbs
1-2 egg yolks
2 tbsps. cream
juice ½ orange
chopped parsley

Method

Put meat in a pan with onion, herbs, peppercorns, cloves and stock.
Bring to the boil and skim.
Simmer two hours or pressure cook for 30 minutes.
Season and strain stock.
Put butter, stock, wine and more herbs in a double pan and bring to the boil.
Reduce liquor rapidly for 10 minutes.
Beat yolks and cream and add gradually without boiling.
Stir in meat with a good squeeze of orange juice.
Serve sprinkled with parsley.

Bere Regis Sausage

Bere Regis is in the heart of Thomas Hardy's country and has a lovely church which contains the tombs of the Turbervilles (D'Urbervilles in Hardy's novel).
This dish is more a meat loaf or terrine than a sausage.

1 lb. minced raw beef
1 lb. minced bacon
6 ozs. fresh breadcrumbs
1 small grated nutmeg
½ tsp. mace
2 beaten eggs
seasoning
toasted crumbs

Method

Mix meats well together.
Stir in crumbs, beaten eggs, spices and seasonings.
Bake in a greased cake or bread tin for 1 ½ hours standing in a water bath at gas 3 or 325°F.
Coat with crumbs when cold.

Note:- cooking in a water bath keeps the meat moist.

Dorset Jugged Steak

1 ½ lbs. shin of beef, cubed
2 tbsps. flour
1 small sliced onion
3 cloves
2 tsps. chopped parsley
2 ½ fl. ozs. red wine
seasoning
4 ozs. sausagemeat
½ cup fresh breadcrumbs
1 small egg
2 tsps. red current jelly
parsley

Method

Toss meat in flour.
Put in casserole with onion, cloves, parsley, wine and water to cover.
Add seasoning and cover.
Cook 2 ½ hours at gas 2 or 300°F.
Mix sausagemeat, crumbs, beaten egg and seasoning.
Roll into very small balls in floured hands.
Poach in boiling water for 10 minutes.
Stir redcurrant jelly into beef.
Add balls and cook uncovered for 15 minutes.
Serve sprinkled with parsley.

Rolled Steak with Dorset Puffs

This is similar to beef olives but the meat is left in one piece.

1 ½-2 lbs. braising steak ¾" thick in one piece
stuffing –
  1 tsp. dripping or lard
  1 cupful fine fresh breadcrumbs
  pinch mixed dried herbs
  seasoning
  1 finely chopped onion
flour
pinch of sugar
dripping
batter –
  1 egg, beaten
  ½ pint milk
  4 ozs. plain flour
  pinch of salt
to serve –
  brown gravy and vegetables

Method

Flatten steak with a rolling pin.
Stuffing – rub fat into crumbs.
Add herbs, seasoning and onion.
Spread over steak, roll up and tie.
Dust with flour and sugar.
Melt a little dripping in meat tin.
Add meat and roast about 1 ½ hours at gas 4 or 350°F.
Make the batter.
Raise the oven temperature to gas 7 or 425°F twenty minutes before end of cooking and add spoonsful of batter to tin with space between.
Bake until puffy.
Serve hot with gravy and vegetables.

Modern Dorset Casserole

This includes red and green peppers which have become popular in British cooking over the last ten years.

1 ½ lbs. stewing beef, 1'' cubes
litle dripping or oil
½ pint water or stock
½ tsp. nutmeg
½ tsp. salt
½ tsp. pepper
½ pint cider or wine
8 ozs. mushrooms
1 red pepper, chopped
1 green pepper, chopped
1 tbsp. tomato purée
1 tbsp. meat or vegetable extract
1 rounded tbsp. flour
Note:— the secret of a good meat casserole is to keep the meat just covered with liquid and to cook it slowly

Method

Toss meat in hot fat or oil until sealed.
Add seasonings, spices, water and cider or wine.
Cover and cook 1 ½ hours at gas 3 or 325°F.
Add mushrooms, peppers, purée and meat or vegetable extract
Blend flour with a little stock or water and stir in.
Continue cooking for about another hour or until meat is tender

Portland Pasties

Similar to Cornish pasties with the addition of turnip and horseradish.

8 ozs. shortcrust pastry
filling: —
4 ozs. raw minced beef
2 tsps. water
6 ozs. grated turnip
4-6 ozs. diced potato
seasoning
1 level tbsp. horseradish sauce
beaten egg glaze

Method

Roll pastry thinly and cut three 6'' rounds. Re-roll pastry and cut another round.
Mix filling ingredients together and season well.
Place filling in centre of rounds.
Damp edges of pastry with egg and fold to make pasty shapes, crimping edges.
Brush with egg and make a small hole for steam.
Bake 15 minutes at gas 6 or 400°F.
Reduce to gas 4 or 350°F for 30 minutes.

*The following two recipes can be cooked in a hay box or its modern equivalent — **a hot box or crockpot.***

Beef Trombton

A piece of flank beef (3-4 lbs.)
8 onions
8 carrots
2 parsnips
2-4 turnips
pinch nutmeg or mace
few cloves
few black peppercorns
seasoning
sauce —
  bunch herbs — thyme, parsley, marjoram
  1 chopped anchovy fillet
  few capers
  thick gravy

Method

Cover beef with water and bring to the boil. Skim.
Add rest of ingredients and stew very slowly for **5 hours!**
A crockpot would be very useful for this or a hot box.
Cook on the stove for the first ½ hour.
Sauce — chop herbs finely and add anchovy and capers.
Bring to the boil in gravy.
Serve hot with the meat.

To Cook a Ham in a Copper

15 lb. ham
cold water to cover
a copper
note — or use a hot box with a smaller ham

Method

Put ham in the copper.
Well cover with water and bring slowly to the boil and boil 20 mins.
Take fire away from underneath and cover copper well with old coats or blankets to keep in heat.
Leave 12 hours or less, according to the size of ham.
Remove from water.

To Jug a Hare

This is an old recipe from the 17th century.

'Cut your Hare in Pieces, season it with Pepper, Salt and Nutmeg, put it into the Jug, with 4 onions, a piece of Bacon, some Cloves, a Quarter of a Pound of Butter, a bunch of sweet herbs and a Bayleaf or two, stop it down close with a cork and paste, then put it into a pot of boyling Water, 4 or 5 Hours take it out of the Jug and put it into a Stew Pan with 2 Anchovies, half a Pint of Claret and stew it a Quarter of an Hour, bruise the liver very well and put it in with the Anchovies, the Butter must be laid first into the Jug.'

Wessex Turkey or Chicken

2 onions
salt
1 turkey leg joint (thigh and drumstick) or
2 chicken legs
4 ozs. ham or cooked bacon
butter
1 rounded tbsp. flour
¼ pint dry cider
pepper
triangles of bread
parsley

Method

Quarter one onion and sprinkle with ½ tsp. salt.
Put in pan with poultry and ½ pint water.
Bring to the boil, cover and simmer about 45 minutes until tender
Remove meat to a plate.
Strain stock and keep.
Chop cooked onion.
Remove skin and bone from poultry and cut meat into large pieces.
Cut ham or bacon in ½'' strips.
Melt 2 ozs. butter and fry other onion, sliced, for 7 minutes.
Add flour and cook 2 minutes.
Stir in cider and ¼ pint of stock.
Bring to the boil.
Add meats and onion and simmer 5 minutes.
Pour into dish.
Fry triangles of bread in butter.
Dip in stock and parsley. Garnish dish

Dorset Rabbit

Rabbits are just as numerous in Dorset as in other counties and can provide a cheap and tasty meal.

6-8 young rabbit joints, soaked in strong salted water overnight.
seasoned flour
6 ozs. streaky bacon
seasoning
2 tbsps. chopped sage
½ cup cider
forcemeat crust —
- 1 lb. onions
- 2 ozs. butter or margarine
- 8 ozs. white breadcrumbs
- grated rind ½ lemon
- 3 tbsps. chopped parsley
- 1 egg

Method

Dry joints well.
Roll in seasoned flour.
Cut bacon in strips and blanch in boiling water for 2 minutes. Drain
Pack joints in a deep casserole with seasoning and sage.
Add cider and scatter on bacon.
Crust — chop onions finely and cook in fat. Cool and add crumbs, rind, parsley and egg to bind.
Spread over rabbit and cook 2 hours at gas 3 or 325°F until brown on top.

PUDDINGS

*Apples feature widely in Dorset cooking as apple trees abound in the gardens.
The following recipes make good use of windfalls.*

Apple Gâteau

2 lb. apple pulp (weight after cooking)
1 ½ lbs. sugar
rind 1 lemon
½ pint water
Note — for a preserve ("cheese") pot in warm, dry jars.

Method

Boil all ingredients together for several hours in a thick based pan until very thick.
Test for a set.
Turn into moulds and serve with cream or custard

Apple Hedgehog

This is a variation of the above recipe.

1 lb. cooking apples, peeled and cored
¾ lb. sugar
½ tsp. nutmeg or ginger
blanched almonds cut in strips
whipped cream or custard

Add enough water to moisten apples in pan.
Add sugar and nutmeg or ginger and boil until mixture drops from a spoon.
Set in a mould.
Turn out and stick all over with almonds
Cover with cream or custard.

Dorset Dumplings

Good with clotted cream but bad for the figure!

4 cooking apples
pastry —
- 8 ozs. self raising flour
- 4 ozs. shredded suet
- pinch salt
- water to mix

4 ozs. demerara sugar
4 ozs. butter or margarine
2 tsps. ground ginger
rum
4 cloves
4 pudding cloths or foil

Method

Peel apples and remove cores keeping apples whole.
Make pastry. Roll and cut in squares.
Mix sugar, butter, ginger and rum to moisten.
Place apples on pastry and fill centres with rum mixture, piling well on top.
Press one clove into each.
Fold up pastry, wetting edges.
Press well together and put each dumpling in well floured cloth or piece of foil.
Drop into boiling water and boil 45 minutes or steam for 1 hour.

Note — dumplings can also be baked in a moderate oven.

Melt in the Mouth Pastry

This amount of pastry will be sufficient for the next three recipes, or alternatively, can be frozen.

½ lb. Spry or Trex
½ lb. soft margarine
3-4 ozs. caster sugar
1 egg
1 ¼ lbs. flour

Method

Cream Spry or Trex with margarine and sugar.
Work in beaten egg and fold in flour.
Knead lightly, wrap and chill at least 5 hours, longer if possible.
Use as required for sweet flans etc.

Dorset Lemon Tart

4-5 ozs. pastry
filling —
    2 large cooking apples
    3 ozs. sugar
    grated rind and juice 1 lemon
    1 egg
7'' flan ring or dish

Method

Roll pastry and line ring or dish.
Filling — peel and grate apples.
Add sugar, lemon rind and juice.
Beat in egg and pour mixture into pastry case.
Bake 45 minutes at gas 4 or 350°F.
Note — stand over glass or china dishes on baking trays while cooking to ensure that the pastry base is cooked.

Treacle Tart

This is more like a mincemeat tart with the addition of golden syrup.

8 ozs. pastry
3 ozs. fresh breadcrumbs
grated rind and juice 1 lemon
1 large cooking apple, grated
6 ozs. mixed dried fruit
¼ tsp. mixed spice
¼ tsp. ground ginger
little caster sugar

Method

Line a pie plate or tin with half of pastry.
Mix rest of ingredients well together and fill plate
Cover with rest of pastry.
Brush with water and sprinkle with sugar
Bake ½ hour at gas 6 or 400° F.
Reduce to gas 4 or 350°F if too brown.

Blueberry Pie

Blueberries are grown commercially in Dorset. Blackberries or blackcurrants may also be used.

8 ozs pastry
filling —
- 1 lb. blueberries
- 1-2 tbsps. sugar
- 1 tbsp. cornflour
- 1 tbsp. lemon juice

topping —
- little water or egg white
- 1 tsp. sugar

to serve —
- clotted cream

Method

Line pie plate with half of pastry.
Mix fruit with sugar and cornflour.
Moisten with lemon juice and place on pastry.
Note — the addition of cornflour will thicken the juices as they cook.
Damp pastry edges and cover with rest of pastry.
Brush top with water or egg white and sprinkle with sugar
Bake ½ hour at gas 6 or 400°F.
Serve with clotted cream.

Dorset Christmas Pudding

10 ozs. flour
10 ozs. fresh breadcrumbs
1 ¼ lbs. shredded suet
½ tsp. salt
10 ozs. brown sugar
¼ oz. mixed spice
2 tsps. grated nutmeg
grated rind 1 lemon
1 ¼ lbs. raisins
1 ¼ lbs. currants
5 ozs. chopped mixed peel
10 eggs
½ cup milk
¼ pint brandy or ale

Method

Grease two large pudding basins.
Mix all dry ingredients well together in a large mixing bowl.
Beat in eggs and brandy or ale with enough milk to make a moist dough.
Put in basins, cover and steam 6-8 hours.
Remove covers and replace with greaseproof paper for storing.
Steam 3-4 hours on Christmas Day

Quaking Pudding

This recipe and the next two use a pint of double cream in each. This may prove expensive unless the home made cream recipe is used.

Blender Cream

½ lb. unsalted butter
½ pint milk
liquidiser, blender or cream machine

Pudding –

3 egg yolks
½ nutmeg, grated
little cinnamon
flour
pinch salt

to serve –

melted butter and sugar

Method

Cut up butter and heat in pan with milk until almost boiling. Leave until blood heat, then blend at maximum for 1 minute or pump through machine. Leave covered in refrigerator overnight.
pudding –
Whip cream, yolks, nutmeg and cinnamon until thick.
Mix in enough flour with salt until really thick.
Wet a strong pudding cloth in hot water and flour well. Put in pudding and tie close. Put in boiling water for 6 hours.
Serve cut across with butter and sugar.

Syllabub

1 pint cream
½ pint red wine
juice of 2 lemons
peel of 1 lemon, grated
sugar to taste

Method

Whip all ingredients well together until thick.
Put in dishes and serve.

Cream Toasts

This is an old 17th century recipe.

3 egg yolks
1 pint cream
sugar
cinnamon
grated lemon peel
¼" slices French bread
1-2 beaten eggs
oil and butter for frying
sugar
orange segments

Method

Mix yolks, cream, grated lemon peel, cinnamon and sugar (to taste) well together.
Soak bread quickly in this mixture, then in beaten egg.
Fry in oil and butter until crisp.
Serve hot with sugar and orange segments.

Sago Cream

Sago was a popular ingredient in puddings as far back as the 17th century.
It seems to have gone out of fashion now and has been replaced bysemolina or ground rice
This old recipe makes a large quantity and can be adapted.

8 ozs. sago
2-3 quarts milk
sugar to taste
cinnamon
1 quart double cream
brown sugar for top

Method

Wash and clean sago well.
Boil it in the milk until very thick and soft. Leave it to get cold.
Mix in sugar to taste with cinnamon.
Stir in cream and put in oven dish.
'You may colour it with a hott Iron' or in modern terms sprinkle with lines of brown sugar and brown under a hot grill

Furmity

Quote from Thomas Hardy –

"It is nourishing and as proper a food as could be obtained within the four seas."
Wheat was gleaned by cottagers, cooked and mixed with any flavouring, sweet or savoury.

To make –

Wash 4 heaped tablespoonsful of best wheat well in several waters, then soak it in water for 24 hours.
Place in a double pan and cover with plenty of milk.
Stew gently about 4 hours until soft and the wheat grain skin is just bursting. Pour off surplus milk and add sugar, raisins, mixed spice, cinnamon or ginger to taste.

BREAD, CAKES and BISCUITS

Wholemeal Bread

This will make 4-5 loaves of delicious bread.
The addition of vitamin C is not essential, but helps to speed the rising of the dough.

3 lbs. wholemeal flour
2 dessps. salt
1 oz. sugar
1-2 ozs. lard
2 ozs. fresh yeast or 1 oz. dried yeast
1 ½-2 pints warm water
50 mg. tablet Vitamin C
4-5 greased bread tins

Method

Warm large bowl, flour and salt.
Dissolve half of sugar and crushed Vitamin C tablet in ½ pint warm water with yeast. Leave in a warm place to froth.
Rub fat into flour, salt and rest of sugar.
Add yeast liquid and rest of water.
Mix and knead for 5 minutes until smooth and soft dough.
Leave to stand for 5 minutes.
Knead again and divide dough into four or five pieces.
Roll dough like a swiss roll and place in warm tins. The dough should come about halfway up the tins. Cover and put to rise to the top of the tins in a warm place.
Meanwhile set the oven to the highest temperature.
Put tins in the oven and reduce temperature to Gas 8 or 450°F.
Bake about 40 minutes. Turn out on to a cooling tray. Loaves should sound hollow when base is tapped.

Portland Dough Cake

Portland is famous for its grey building stone and the Verne Prison.

1 lb. enriched bread dough (made with 1 egg and milk instead of water)
6 ozs. soft brown sugar
½ tsp. mixed spice
¼ tsp. nutmeg
1 lb. currants
10 ozs. lard or margarine
8 ozs. plain flour

Method

Bread dough should be risen.
Work all the ingredients into the risen dough.
Put in a warm place to rise for 30 minutes.
Drop dough into a round greased tin and bake 40 minutes at gas 6 or 400°F

Dorset Dough Cake

12 ozs. plain flour
pinch salt
1 tsp. mixed spice
3 ozs. margarine
½ oz. fresh yeast
3 ozs. sugar
7½ fl. ozs. warm milk
2 eggs
4 ozs. currants
2 ozs. sultanas

Method

Sieve and warm flour, salt and spice.
Rub fat into flour.
Cream yeast with 1 teaspoon of sugar.
Add half of warmed to yeast and pour on to sieved ingredients.
Leave in a warm place to rise about ½ hour.
Add rest of milk and beaten eggs with rest of sugar and beat well.
Leave in a warm place to double about 1 hour.
Beat in fruit and put in greased cake tin.
Prove in warm place for 25-30 minutes.
Bake 45 minutes at gas 5 or 375°F.

Dorset Teabread

Dorset tea breads are not made with yeast and can be sweet or savoury.

Savoury Dorset Teabread

4 ozs. finely chopped bacon
2 chopped cooking apples
small grated onion
little margarine
8 ozs. self raising flour
1 tsp. salt
½ tsp. pepper
1 oz. lard or bacon fat
2 ozs. grated cheese
1 egg
5 tbsps. milk

Method

Fry bacon, apples and onion gently in little margarine until soft. Cool.
Sieve flour, salt and pepper.
Rub in fat, then stir in bacon mix.
Beat egg and milk and stir in with cheese.
Spoon into greased bread tin.
Bake 40 minutes at gas 5 or 375°F.
Serve sliced and buttered.

Dorset Bara Brith (or tea bread)

This is still served in a tea shop in Abbotsbury, a village famous for its Swannery which dates back at least to 1393.

12 ozs. mixed dried fruit
12 ozs. sugar
¾ pint cold tea
1 beaten egg
1 lb. self raising flour
8″ greased square tin

Method

Soak fruit and sugar in cold tea overnight.
Next day beat in egg and flour.
Pour into greased tin and bake
1-1 ½ hours at gas 5 or 375°F.
Slice and butter when cold.

Blackmore Vale Cake

The Vale of Blackmore in North Dorset has dairy farms on lush, heavy clay soil with lanes between wide grass verges and hedgerows.

This cake has always been served to the Blackmore Vale Hunt for over 100 years.

4 ozs. butter or margarine
4 ozs. caster sugar
bare ½ pint warm milk
2 tsps. treacle or molasses
1 tsp. bicarbonate of soda
12 ozs. plain flour
12 ozs. raisins
3 ozs. chopped peel
6″ greased and lined cake tin

Method

Cream fat and sugar until light.
Mix milk, soda and treacle or molasses.
Add flour gradually to creamed mixture alternatively with milk mixture, beating well.
Fold in raisins and peel.
Bake 1 ¼-1 ½ hours at gas 3 or 325°F

Dorset Apple Cake

Probably the most famous of Dorset recipes.

½ lb. cooking apples, peeled, cored and chopped
4 ozs. sugar
8 ozs. plain flour
pinch salt
1 ½ tsps. baking powder
4 ozs. margarine or lard
1 egg or 3 tbsps. milk
Optional — 2 tbsps. dried fruit
butter
7-8'' sandwich tin, greased

Method

Mix apples with sugar.
Sieve flour, salt and baking powder.
Rub in fat.
Stir apples into flour mixture with dried fruit if used.
Mix to a firm dough with beaten egg or milk.
Spread into tin about 1'' thick.
Bake 45-50 minutes at gas 4 or 350°F.
Serve hot, cut through and spread with butter.

Matrimony Cake or Pie

On Midsummer Eve girls would put apple pips on the fire. If the pip burned it meant her lover was false, but if the pip burst, her lover was true.
This cakes includes apples, but no pips and is more a tart than a cake, dating from about 1800.

8 ozs. shortcrust pastry
2 large cooking apples, cored, peeled and cut in rings
4 tbsps. fresh breadcrumbs
4 tbsps. mixed dried fruit
½ tsp. nutmeg and ground ginger mixed
juice 1 lemon
2 tbsps. sugar
2 tbsps. golden syrup
1 lemon slice
little milk
to serve — clotted cream
8'' flan tin or dish

Method

Roll half of pastry and line tin.
Cover with apple rings, overlapping.
Add rest of ingredients well mixed.
Place a slice of lemon in centre.
Cover with rest of pastry, damping edges to seal.
Brush with milk and bake about ½ hour at gas 5 or 375°F.
Serve hot with cream.

Dorset Pot Cake

This is cooked in a deep frying pan.

Fresh fruit, such as apple slices, gooseberries or blackcurrants can be used instead of dried fruit.

1 egg
8 fl. ozs. milk
3 ozs. butter or margarine
3 ozs. lard
12 ozs. plain flour
3 ozs. sugar
6 ozs. currants
6 ozs. sultanas
butter
2 well greased frying pans
variation —
  12 ozs. fresh fruit
  demerara sugar

Method

Beat egg and milk together.
Rub fats into flour.
Add sugar and dried fruit.
Mix to a dough with egg and milk.
Grease and heat frying pan.
Pour in mixture, reduce heat and cook very slowly until brown.
Reverse into another frying pan and cook until second side is brown.
Cut open and spread with butter.
With fresh fruit, add demerara sugar with butter when serving.

Dorset Fluffy Cakes

These are made with cornflour which gives them a light fluffy texture.

6 ozs. butter or margarine
4 ozs. caster sugar
8 ozs. cornflour
1 tsp. baking powder
2 beaten eggs
3 drops vanilla essence
patty tins

Method

Cream fat and sugar until pale and fluffy.
Mix in sieved cornflour and baking powder.
Beat in eggs and vanilla essence.
Grease tins and half fill with mixture.
Bake 15 minutes at gas 6 or 400°F.

Charminster Cheese Cakes

4 ozs. shortcrust pastry
2 ozs. butter or margarine
2 ozs. caster sugar
1 beaten egg
1 tsp. almond essence
2 ozs. ground rice
1 oz. currants
patty tins

Method

Line 12 patty tins with pastry.
Cream fat and sugar until light and fluffy.
Gradually beat in egg and essence.
Fold in ground rice and currants.
Threequarters fill pastry cases.
Bake 20 minutes at gas 6 or 400°F.

Dorset Fair Gingerbreads

Markets and fairs are still popular in Dorset and home made gingerbreads sell "like hot cakes."

6 ozs. black treacle
5 ozs. butter or margarine
6 ozs. plain flour
6 ozs. dark brown sugar
1 tsp. ground ginger

Method

Warm treacle gently without boiling.
Rub fat into flour and mix in sugar and ginger
Beat in warmed treacle.
Drop small pieces well apart on greased tins.
Bake ½ hour at gas 3 or 325°F.

Chocolate Brownies

2 ozs. plain chocolate
3 ozs. margarine or butter
2 ozs. caster sugar
1 egg
4 ozs. self raising flour
¼ tsp. salt
3 ozs. chopped walnuts
little milk
caster sugar
Swiss roll tin

Method

Melt chocolate in a basin over hot water.
Cream fat and sugar until light.
Beat in egg and sieve in flour and salt.
Stir in nuts and melted chocolate with enough milk to make a soft dough.
Spread in greased tin and dredge top with caster sugar.
Bake ½ hour at gas 4 or 350°F.
Cut in squares while warm and leave to cool in tin.

Dorset Shortbread

This is easy to make and has a crunchy edging.

12 ozs. plain flour
4 ozs. icing sugar
8 ozs. butter
demerara sugar
Note — the uncooked biscuit roll can be frozen

Method

Knead flour, butter and icing sugar together until smooth.
Form into long sausage shapes and roll in demerara sugar.
Cut in ¼'' slices and bake 10-15 minutes at gas 4 or 350°F, on lightl greased baking tins.

Dorset Easter Biscuits

12 ozs. butter or margarine
8 ozs. caster sugar
3 egg yolks
1 lb. plain flour
1 tsp. mixed spice or cinnamon
3 ozs. currants

Method

Cream fat and sugar until light.
Beat in egg yolks gradually.
Fold in sieved flour and spice or cinnamon.
Stir in currants. Knead slightly.
Roll mixture very thinly on floured board.
Cut in 3'' rounds with fluted cutter.
Prick and bake on greased tins about 20 minutes at gas 4 or 350°F.

MISCELLANEOUS

Dorset Knobs

These are semi-sweet rusk type biscuits or small rolls.
They are made to a secret recipe by Moores of Morecombelake.
They are best eaten with a very little butter and Blue Vinney cheese.

Blue Vinney Cheese

This cheese named after "vinid" which means mouldy, has become very scarce and is made in just a very few farmhouses in Dorset. It is made with simple equipment and skim milk, not separated milk as the cheese requires some fat.

4 gallons of milk from the day before with some of the cream hand skimmed. Raise the milk to 85°F then add 2-3 teaspoonsful of cheese-making rennet. Keep at this temperature until the curd separates, then cut the curd with the hand. Drain the whey from the bucket, crumble the curd into pieces the size of a small nut, then add ½ ounce of salt for each pound of curd. Pack into moulds lined with wet muslin and put to press lightly for 24 hours. Store on a stone floor and turn the cheeses every day. Leave up to 4 months by this time they should have "blued".

Clotted Cream

"Take the night's milk and put into a broad earthenware pan and in the morning set over a slow fire letting it stand there from morning to night, suffering it not to boil, only heat. Then take off the heat and set it in some place to cool all night and next morning dish off your cream and it will be very thick".

Dorset Moss or Dorset Weed

Vegetable gelatine contains iodine and other valuable salts.
Valuable for gland troubles and children with adenoids or sore throats (made hot as a drink).

Gathered in April or May from the seas when light brown or bleached on the shore. Wash well in running brook water and spread out to dry on grass. Keep pouring buckets of fresh water over or leave out in the rain. When bleached a creamy white, trim off rough places, stalks etc. Give it a final wash, dry it thoroughly until it is reall crisp. Store in bags hung in a dry place. Will keep indefinitely if properly prepared. If some salt remains in it, it will pick up damp.

Apple Mincemeat

This makes a delicious filling for cooked pastry flans and tarts.

1 lb. eating apples
1 lb. mixed dried fruit
12 ozs. chopped peel
¼ pint cider
¼ pint water
½ tsp. ground ginger
¼ tsp. ground nutmeg
¾ lb. sugar
juice of 1 small lemon
½ tsp. almond essence

Method

Peel, core and dice apples.
Butter a pan and add apples, dried fruit, peel, cider and water.
Cook gently for 20 minutes.
Mix spices and sugar and add lemon juice.
Add to fruit mix and boil 20 minutes.
Cool and add essence.
Pot and cover.

Posset

1 pint cream
rind 2 lemons, grated
1 pint white wine
2 egg whites, lightly beaten

Method

Mix all ingredients well together and serve in glasses.

Damson or Sloe Gin

1 pint gin
12-18 sloes or damsons
12 bay leaves
2 ozs. sugar

Method

Prick fruit and add to gin.
Put in an earthenware jar with bay leaves and sugar. Cork well and leave three weeks. Test and add more sugar if necessary.
Leave one year before draining and bottling.

Dorset Tea Wine

4 pints cold tea saved from teapot
2 lbs. sugar
8 ozs. raisins
2 lemons

Method

Chop raisins and slice lemons thinly.
Put in bowl with sugar and pour on tea.
Stir until sugar is dissolved. Cover.
Leave 1 month, then remove scum, strain and bottle.
Keep in a dark cool place lightly corked for 3-4 months.

Metheglin (or White Ale)

Economic if you keep bees!

5 lbs. honey
1 gallon water
1 lemon
1 sprig of rosemary
1 sprig balm
½ oz. root ginger
¾ oz. fresh baker's yeast or mead yeast
variations —
use orange instead of lemon
use cloves, cinnamon, marjoram, balm or hops

Method

Simmer herbs and spices with thin lemon rind in water for 20 minutes.
Strain and pour on to honey.
Stir well to dissolve honey.
When lukewarm add juice of lemon and yeast.
Cover and leave to ferment 24 hours.
Pour into fermentation jar with air lock. Leave to ferment to a finish in a warm place.
Remove to a cooler place for 3 weeks before syphoning into storage jars.

Dorset Apple Wine

Another good use for windfalls

3½ lbs. cooking apples
1½ gallons cold water
3 lbs. sugar
2 lemons
1 orange

Method

Cut up and core apples without peeling.
Put in a large bowl and pour cold water over. Leave a week stirring every day with a wooden spoon.
Strain liquid off through muslin.
Add sugar and juice with grated rinds of lemons and orange.
Stir well until sugar is dissolved.
Cover and leave 24 hours. Strain and bottle. Cork loosely until it has stopped working.

Rum Punch

A warm welcome for Christmas guests.

2 pints boiling water
rind and juice 1 lemon
rind and juice 2 oranges
8 ozs. sugar
1 pint rum
strips of angelica and glacé cherries or
maraschino cherries

Method

Pour boiling water over thinly pared lemon rind. Add juice of lemon and oranges and grated rind of 1 orange.
Add sugar and infuse in a warm place.
Add rum and heat.
Serve in a punch bowl with angelica and cherries.

INDEX